EXCELLENCE

IN

ATTITUDE

By Robb Thompson

Excellence in Attitude
ISBN 1-889723-25-8
Copyright © 2002 by Robb Thompson
Family Harvest Church
18500 92nd Ave.
Tinley Park, Illinois 60477

Editorial Consultant: Cynthia Hansen
Text Design: Lisa Simpson
Cover Design: Greg Lane

DEDICATION

This book is dedicated to all those who by hot pursuit have chosen an excellent attitude — in spite of those who by their poor attitude may never affect anyone in a positive way.

A SPECIAL THANK YOU
TO THESE *WINNING IN LIFE* PARTNERS
FOR HELPING ME TAKE THIS BOOK
AROUND THE WORLD:

Abi Adeleke
Mark & Colleen Aitkenhead
Walter Aldape
Kenneth Anczerewicz
Mary Arrigoni
Maureen Barone
Teresa Barrera
Roceal Beauford
Gloria Beckley
James & Geraldine Bell
Barbara Bentley
John & Kim Berberich
Jean Biela
Kevin & Regina Blacke
Debbie Blay
Douglas & Markay Boettcher
Michael Boettcher
Alana Boettcher
Bryan Boettcher
Sandra Briggs
Jeff Brown
Michael & Yvounda Brown
Les & Barbara Burdsal
William & Joyce Butler
Steven & Lorna Carrara
Darryl Chang
MaryAnn Cherry
Penny Christian
Michael & Rose Clancy

Ron & Tamara Collum
Sheri Crosby
Glenda Crosby
Enrique & Christina Cruz
James & Terese Cruz
Michael Daidone
Steve & Christine De Young
Mark & Mary Dempsey
Ed Diaz
Nathaniel & Leola Douglas
Victoria Dowdy
Ramon & Hilda Dros
Neil Dubreuil
Debra Dunbar
Robert & Wendy Durham
Robert & Taylor Durling
Marsha Easter
Marvin Edwards
William J. Elliott
Joe & Vanessa Ellis
Elmer & Wendy Embry
Randy Emrick
Dr. George Fabre, Sr.
Susan Faro
Julie Fenner
Mitchell Ferguson
Virginia Ferry
Richard & Margaret Flores
Darren & Mary Freihage

Mark & Donna Friend
Rebeca Gaode
Angela Gayden
Paul & Pam Geallis
Nathan & Connie Giffin
George Gilmer
Ticinia Glass
Ruby Gordon-Penny
Jeffrey & Kris Griffiths
Kris Griffiths
Christine Grishom
Shantini Gunasegaram
Lauren Gunther
Mary Joan Gunther
Foyla Hall
Christina Hardy
Sharolyn Hardy
Eddie & Sissy Hartsell
Ed & Deanna Hauschild
Zhavonne Haynes
Arlene Henderson
Greg & Stephanie Henthorn
Jennifer Henzler
Cindy Highley
Dan Hochgesang
Ruby Hougham
Al & Sandra Houston
Jane Jarosz
Rosemary Johnson
Gloria Johnson
Justin & Sarah Kane
Robert Kelm
Dale & Laura Kerouac
Joseph Kestel
William & Dianne Knapp
Raymond & Mignon La Vigne
Phil & Mary Lambert

Ralph Laplanche
Michael Leslie
Joe Linder
Michael & Rebecca Lopez
Dorothy Lowe
Martin & Carole Lumbert
Yvette Lyda
Hosea & Lahomia Lyles
Scott & Nancy Mac Ritchie
Steve & Sherise Marinich
Corey & Kim Marsh
Jean Martin
John & Ana Luisa Martinez
Anna Marie Martusciello
Robert & Carolyn Mason
Gale & Elizabeth Mathus
Sheila Mays
Patrick & Tamara Mc Collum
Catherine Mc Intosh
Marlene Mc Kane
Benjamin & Sandra Medina
Frank & Joanne Miller
Barbara Molek
Lyle & Charmaine Moore
Gloria Lee Morgan
Brenda Nelson
Thomas & Anna Nestor
Brenda O'Neal
Thomas & Veronica O'Neill
Cheryl Onyemena
Steve Osborn
Javier & Julia Palos
David Parson
Lula Perine
Joseph & Susan Petrovic
Lisa Quinn
Judith Ramsay

Misy Read
Karen Reed
Amanda Reeves
Patty Ridings
Oralia Rodriguez
Joey Rogers
Yolanda Romanazzi
Jennifer Romanowski
Samuel & Sharon Ross
William & Kristine Ross
Milton & Velma Rouse
Richard & Diane Rozich
James Rucker
Eugene & Gilda Santor
Betty Savage
Warren & Linda Shafer
Nancy Shannon
Steve & Megan Shapiro
Chris & Cindy Shefts
Thomas & Sherri Socco
Michelle Solis
Helen Smith
Joy Smith
Jamie Spada
Michael & Roberta Spencer
Anthony Stanfield
Shirley Stanley
Holly Stasiak
La Verne Stemmons
Emily Jean Stinnett
Susan Stinnett
David Stinnett
Patricia Styles
Ray & Stephanie Tamayo
Wilbert Taylor

Diana Taylor
Leonard & Geraldine Thomas
Tonia Thomas
Cherylyn Thompson
Linda Thompson
Thomas & Lisa Tichy
Sara Toledo
Cecelia Torres
Wilfredo Torres
Dale Travis
Rachel Trimble
John & Christine Van Horn
Bill & Peggy Vander Velde
Juan Vargas
Richard & Donna Varno
Anthony Ventrice
Phyllis Vickery
Judy Vinsant
Rick & Bette Wagner
Velma Walker
Susan Watley
Tasha Weatherspoon
Athens & Sharon Weed
Richard & Susan Wegman
Dale Wiggins
Thomas Wiggins
Chuck & Melody Willett
Darrell & Patsy Williams
Milton Wilson
Samuel & Deborah Woods
Grace Yeager
Akberet Yohannes
Zachariah Zayner
Judy Zotos
In Memory of Tony Kellem

TABLE OF CONTENTS

Introduction

INTRODUCTION

This world we live in has so marred and camouflaged what is right before God that the great majority of people don't even know how to live their lives. They have no idea how to become what God wants them to become.

There is only one way to change this sad situation, and it's found in the Word of God. Only God's Word gives us a true picture of the way life is really supposed to be. If we are ever going to find out what is right before the Lord in every area of life, we must take a look at the Scriptures and find out the differences between what God says and what society says. These are the differences that give us our significance in life.

The challenge many people face is that they place their highest priority on being liked and accepted by others. To that end, they make sure they look like everyone else. They dress like everyone else. They drive the same cars as everyone else. They do their jobs like everyone else.

But we will be never remembered, pursued, or rewarded, by that which makes us the same as those around us. We will only be remembered because of our differences.

What is it that makes you different, friend? Whatever it is, that is the quality which will get you noticed by those who can promote you in life. *And nothing will get you noticed more quickly than an excellent attitude.* Why is that? Because there are so few people left in this world who have an excellent attitude! Everyone *wants* excellence, but few are willing to do what is necessary to *achieve* it.

What about you? Are you willing to pay the price for excellence in your life? If so, you must take inventory of the way you've been thinking. You see, the word "attitude" refers to *a posture that is assumed by your body in connection with a feeling or a mood.* Attitude also refers to *a way of thinking that is demonstrated in your disposition, demeanor, and opinion.* When you have an attitude about a certain subject, that attitude is displayed in the way you approach people and talk to them about the subject. Your demeanor and your words will always reflect your attitude.

When you rule your attitudes, you rule your own heart. That is extremely significant, because the Bible says a person who can rule his own spirit is greater than he who can take a city (Prov. 16:32). Think of it — if you learn how to rule your attitudes, you become greater in God's eyes than a four-star general with an army at his command who is able to take an entire city by force!

That's why maintaining an excellent attitude is so very important. In fact, in the arena of excellence, attitude is almost everything.

The moment you ignore your poor attitudes is the moment you take a wrong turn that leads to mediocrity and defeat. So once you make the decision to pursue excellence at all costs, don't ever try to bypass this very basic step. Deal with a poor attitude every time it rears its ugly head. Become known for your excellent attitude, and then watch as God opens doors of opportunity to propel you into a life where winning is an everyday event!

Robb Thompson

EMBRACING LIFE WITH AN EXCELLENT ATTITUDE

Do you want to push beyond mediocrity and attain excellence in every area of your life? If you do, you must take inventory of the way you think. *If you rule your mind, you will rule your life.*

For instance, let's start with the most basic questions. How do you approach life? What is the attitude you carry into the situations and challenges you encounter on a daily basis?

How you respond to these fundamental questions is critical, for your life will only reflect excellence if you continually maintain an attitude of excellence. Therefore, I want to share several principles with you that you must understand in order to take control of your poor attitudes and move toward your goal of ever-increasing excellence in every area of life.

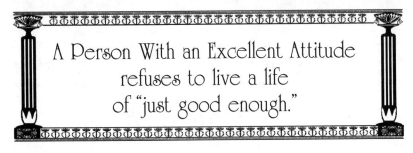

A Person With an Excellent Attitude
refuses to live a life
of "just good enough."

Many people think "good enough" is acceptable. But it *isn't* acceptable if you want to become a person of excellence.

A person of excellence refuses to limit his expectations of life and of himself to "just good enough." He is always motivating himself to become better, to rise higher, to achieve more.

Actually, one of the greatest enemies of excellence is the "just-good-enough" attitude. That attitude leads us straight toward mediocrity, which is the opposite of excellence.

To be mediocre is to be frail, inadequate, inferior, substandard, second class, unsatisfactory, commonplace, and ordinary. This is the place where most people want to live their entire lives because it's the place of least resistance and requires the least effort. But "ordinary" is also the greatest hindrance keeping people from becoming what God wants them to become.

You just have to accept the fact that your pursuit of excellence will always make you a little bit different than most other people. But let me help you here. You don't have to be awesome; you just have to stay a step ahead!

That's what excellence is — staying at least one step ahead of ordinary. It doesn't take a lot; it just takes one step. It's like a foot race. In order to beat the competition, all you have to do is be a fraction of a second faster. But after you have won the race, your challenge is to make sure you don't lose your edge in all the races that are yet to come. That's what makes you excellent — learning to stay in that place of victory.

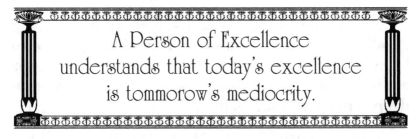

A Person of Excellence understands that today's excellence is tommorow's mediocrity.

You see, excellence is its own standard of competition. This means that continual change is a requirement, not an option, in the pursuit of excellence. Compromise and the status quo are only acceptable to the mediocre — to those who have let their "just-good-enough" attitude keep them in a place called ordinary.

Friend, don't ever let yourself stay for a moment in that place where mediocrity reigns. Make sure your level of excellence tomorrow is always greater than your level of excellence today. "Good enough" should never be good enough for you!

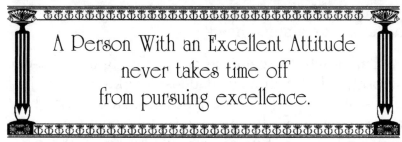

A Person With an Excellent Attitude
never takes time off
from pursuing excellence.

A person who maintains an excellent attitude is an individual who continually presses, presses, presses, presses, and presses for more. He presses his way through obstacles. He is always reaching for a higher level of excellence in every area of life.

We should never let ourselves stop pursuing excellence, even after we've reached the goal we've been striving for. That's the time to start all over again, reaching for a higher level, a greater goal, a deeper purpose than before.

A poor attitude says, "Hey, I've been working hard at pursuing excellence. I deserve a little 'down time' to do whatever I want." But that isn't what God says in His Word. The truth is, there is no "down time" to enjoy a dose of mediocrity if we want to be people of excellence!

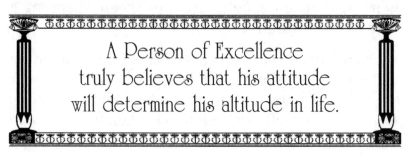

A Person of Excellence
truly believes that his attitude
will determine his altitude in life.

The level of excellence I pursue in my life will determine the altitude God will get out of my life. This is the attitude I carry into every situation of life. I'm convinced that if I press toward excellence — if I continually reach for a higher level of excellence in every area — God will have His way in my life. I'm convinced He will never quit on me; therefore. I will go as far as I can go in fulfilling what God has called me to do.

Now, in order to maintain this attitude toward life, *we have to understand the difference between success and popularity.* Success has to do with the *quality* of life a person lives, whereas popularity has to do with the *quantity* of life a person lives.

Personally, I'm not interested in popularity. A person who is popular will one day have to deal with the fact that he isn't popular anymore. In fact, the day a person becomes popular is just one day closer to the day people begin to reject him. That's why popularity isn't the right goal to pursue.

I recently had the opportunity to see a particular gentleman I went to high school with. This man was a very popular athlete in high school, and he was good at what he did. But you should see him now! Life has not been kind to him! He's seventy pounds overweight and works at a menial job.

Now, I have no problems with a person working at a little Mr. Fixit job, as long as his goal is to own his own business one day with thirty trucks and forty "Mr. Fixits" working for him! He might start out with one truck, but that doesn't mean he's going to stop there. God is bringing him through that stage of his business; He isn't bringing him to that stage so he can say, "That's it. I'm not going any further." No matter where a person starts out in any area of life, that isn't where God wants that person to end.

Anyway, there stood this man — seventy pounds overweight and trudging along in life with a menial job. Nevertheless, he still treated me condescendingly, just as he had when I was in high school!

I looked at this man and realized an important truth: Some people in this world were brought to a particular place in life just by virtue of where and how they grew up, who their parents were, what their parents taught them, and a couple of breaks here and there. But the truly successful individuals in life are those who may have not started out with any advantages; yet these same individuals have made a very honest and accurate evaluation of themselves and then pressed through to become people of excellence.

We have to choose which type of people we're going to be. Are we going to start off in life at the level to which our momma and daddy brought us, only to descend into a life of one disappointment after another where we spend our time blaming the rest of the world for what has happened to us? Or are we going to be people for whom today is always the lowest point of the rest of our lives?

If you choose to be the latter type of person, then today is always the day you say, "I'm going to go further. I'm not going to quit. I'm going to press on. I'm going to press through. I am going to reach for God's highest. I'm going to be everything He has called me to be!"

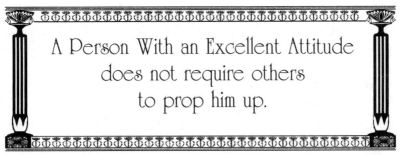

A Person With an Excellent Attitude
does not require others
to prop him up.

A person of excellence is prosperous in his own soul. Therefore, he never has to be propped up by another because he is already a whole person.

With that in mind, let me stress this point: We should never enter an intimate relationship or marry someone who isn't already whole. If we do, we will consistently have to prop up that person and try to make him feel better.

The truth is, we can only prop up people for so long before we have to let them settle wherever they are going to settle in life. After a while, we have to let them deal with their own problems and issues themselves. Meanwhile, we need to make sure we are prospering in our own souls. That way we'll be able to relate *through* other people rather than *to* them.

That's what I do. I endeavor to look through every situation I face. I ask myself, *Why is this person saying what he is saying? Why is he acting the way he is acting? Why did this person do what he did? What is really going on here?*

Then I make the decision that no matter what another person says or does, I will never let his words or actions change my own standard of excellence. I will never let myself be disqualified because of my relationship with someone else.

We don't need other people to prop us up in life. God promises to deliver us from difficult situations as we trust Him and maintain an excellent attitude. The Bible says in Second Peter 2:9 that the Lord knows how to deliver the godly, and that includes every one of us!

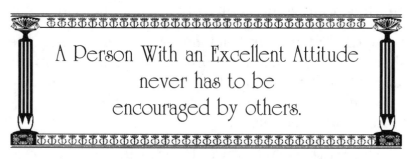

A Person With an Excellent Attitude never has to be encouraged by others.

A person with an excellent attitude never has to be encouraged; instead, he is always searching for someone he can encourage. Meanwhile, he has learned to encourage himself as David did when faced with a great personal crisis.

First Samuel 30 relates the time when enemies captured David's own wife and children, as well as the families of his men. In the terrible emotion of that moment, his men were even talking about stoning him! Yet even in this crisis, David's heart turned toward God:

Now David was greatly distressed, for the people spoke of stoning him, because the soul of all the people was grieved, every man for his sons and his daughters. but David strengthened himself in the Lord his God.

1 Samuel 30:6

David was a man with an excellent attitude. He didn't go around looking for someone to encourage him in the midst of a crisis. The Bible says he encouraged himself in the Lord.

Do you know why it's important to respond to discouraging situations the way David did? Because when you encourage yourself in the Lord, you know you're getting it done right. When other people encourage you, they may make some foolish statements in a misguided effort to make you feel better. Meanwhile, you may be thinking, *I know this person is trying to encourage me, but he really stinks at it!* Of course, you wouldn't want to tell that person, "You're failing miserably at encouraging me," so you just have to stay there and listen to him!

Then there are the people in life who would never think of telling you the truth; they just want to make you feel better. That doesn't help you either. Proverbs 27:6 says, **"Faithful are the wounds of a friend, but the kisses of an enemy are deceitful."**

Of course, you should be thankful for any encouragement you receive. Nevertheless, you need to make a practice of encouraging yourself in the Lord whenever you face obstacles and challenges. You'll always be the one who knows how to do it right.

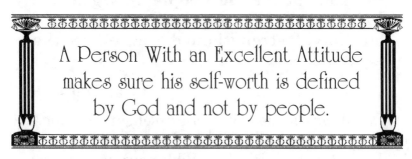

A Person With an Excellent Attitude makes sure his self-worth is defined by God and not by people.

My self-worth doesn't have anything to do with what someone thinks about me, because even if that person loves me today, tomorrow he may not like me at all. People's opinions and affections often change, but God always remains the same. That's why I don't allow my self-worth to be defined by any person; it has to be defined by God and His Word.

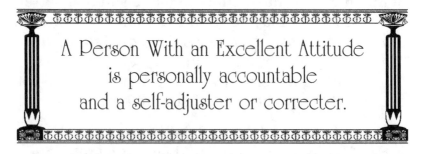

A Person With an Excellent Attitude is personally accountable and a self-adjuster or correcter.

A person of excellence is personally accountable for any wrong thoughts, feelings, or actions he might experience. Therefore, he adjusts within himself when he recognizes something in his life that needs to change.

When you maintain an excellent attitude, you know when you have allowed yourself to dwell on a particular thought pattern that you never should have allowed. You know when you say things you never should have said. And when you recognize you have done something wrong, you deal with it. You are personally accountable, a self-adjuster. You fix the problem. You don't allow yourself to become a negative, complaining, or mediocre person.

I personally cannot bear mediocrity because God cannot bear it. I love the mediocre, but I hate mediocrity. If a person is around me for any length of time, he will either stop being mediocre, or he will stop coming around me, concluding that I'm too judgmental or or that I expect too much of him. Or worst of all, he may think that he is being controlled or manipulated by someone else's standards.

But the truth is, I don't have to say a word to someone who is always wanting to be better. A person who is continually moving toward a greater level of excellence continually corrects himself.

We must never force anyone to the point of having to confront us because of our lack of performance. Instead, we must be our own self-adjusters.

We are the ones who should notify ourselves whenever we're doing something wrong. We know when there is something in our lives that needs to change. When the problem comes to our attention, we need to deal with it immediately rather than just accept it as "the way we are."

You see, the moment we begin to compromise God's standards in our lives is the moment we begin to face increasing challenges. That is also the moment we begin to force other people to become tremendously longsuffering with us.

"Well, they're supposed to forgive me; they're Christians!" we might be tempted to say. That may be true, but it is never left up to us to decide when a person is supposed to forgive us.

This is why: *Forgiveness is in the power of the forgiver, not in the complaint of the person who needs to be forgiven.*

I've often had people come to me and say, "Pastor, if I'm doing anything wrong, I want you to tell me right now."

Immediately I wonder, *To what level does this person want me to take that request?* After all, it's always possible to find some areas in a person's life that need to be corrected because no one has reached perfection yet.

Invariably, even the most well-intentioned Christians get hurt when you tell them that they're doing something wrong in their lives. People just don't like being told that something about them needs to change.

Personally, I embrace those times that I'm told I'm wrong. I didn't say I liked those times, but I don't cry when I go through them either (although I may cry when I get alone in my car!). I also don't try to turn the tables on that person by saying, "Yes, but what about you? Look at what you're doing! You ought to look at yourself in the mirror!"

The fact that I may be doing something wrong has nothing to do with what someone else might be doing wrong in his life. And just because someone "pushes my button" by pointing out what he sees as my problem, that doesn't give me the right to say, "Okay, now it's my turn. These are the things *you're* doing wrong!" If I did that, the conversation would end with absolutely nothing getting accomplished. No, I want to embrace correction, because I want to become a little better every day.

That's why we should be the ones correcting ourselves rather than waiting for someone else to do it. We know better than anyone else when we're doing something wrong, and no one except us can decide to change.

And change we must. It's the only way to escape a life where ordinary is good enough and commonplace describes each day that we live. If we want to live an abundant life of more than enough, we have to change our old ways of thinking and start approaching every situation of life as people with excellent attitudes!

PRINCIPLES FOR EMBRACING LIFE WITH AN ATTITUDE OF EXCELLENCE

★ A Person With an Excellent Attitude refuses to live a life of "just good enough."

★ A Person of Excellence understands that today's excellence is tomorrow's mediocrity.

★ A Person With an Excellent Attitude never takes time off from pursuing excellence.

★ A Person of Excellence truly believes that his attitude will determine his altitude in life.

★ A Person With an Excellent Attitude does not require others to prop him up.

★ A Person With an Excellent Attitude never has to be encouraged by others.

★ A Person With an Excellent Attitude makes sure his self-worth is defined by God and not by people.

★ A Person With an Excellent Attitude is personally accountable and a self-adjuster or corrector.

NOTES:

_____

_____

_____

NOTES:

_____

_____

_____

_____

_____

_____

_____

_____

_____

_____

_____

_____

_____

_____

_____

_____

_____

_____

RELATING TO OTHERS WITH AN EXCELLENT ATTITUDE

Nowhere are your attitudes tested more than in your relationships with other people. After all, it's a lot easier to stay agreeable when the only opinion you have to agree with is your own!

That's why I want to show you some scriptural principles regarding this all-important subject of relating to others. When these principles are followed, they will distinguish you as a person with an excellent attitude in your daily interactions with those around you.

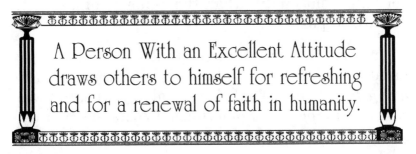

A Person With an Excellent Attitude draws others to himself for refreshing and for a renewal of faith in humanity.

Your attitude, whether good or bad, will affect every individual you come in contact with. That's so important to understand, because you always live in the memory of a person's last encounter with you.

Now think for a moment about a person in your life with whom your last encounter was painful. What is likely to happen the next time you see that person? You may unconsciously put up walls to block communication before he even has an opportunity to open his mouth! Why? Because you remember how you felt the last time he left your presence, and you don't want to repeat the experience!

On the other hand, you will be quick to invite a person with an excellent attitude to go deeper in relationship with you. After talking to that person, you'll spend a few extra minutes at your desk thinking, *You know, that was really nice. I just love talking to him. Every time I do, I'm encouraged. Just the way he approaches life in general encourages me. He's like a breath of fresh air!*

A person with an excellent attitude comes into your life looking for what he can do for *you*, not trying to find out what you can do for *him*. That's a very different quality than the majority of people in this world possess.

In fact, the first thought that often crosses my mind when someone calls me is, *How much is this going to cost me?* That doesn't always mean it will cost me financially. Sometimes it costs me emotionally.

Many times when I pick the telephone, it's almost as if a ringer goes off in the back of my mind, signaling to me that it's time to wrestle. You see, it's a *commitment* to talk to some people, not a privilege or a pleasure — and that commitment can cost dearly at times.

But there are also people in my life who always have an excellent attitude. I can hardly wait to talk to these people. They solve problems for me. They talk to me about my value — the things that are right about me. They make me feel better about being me! They don't flatter me in order to get something from me. They compliment in order to *give* something *to* me.

You don't ever mind inviting that kind of person to come closer to you. You can rest assured that this isn't one of those relationships where the closer you get, the more problems you have to tolerate. You won't have to alter your personality in order to stay in relationship with this individual. Unlike some people, he's not just a trial waiting to happen.

No, as you get closer to a person of excellence, you see more sweetness, not more problems. You can be yourself with him. The more you get to know him, the more you like him. He is an inviting person, someone you want to be around.

When you have an excellent attitude, you invite people to come to you. They just naturally want to be around you! They want to take a closer look at you because they can't figure you out. "What is it about you that's so different?" they ask. "How can you have such a good attitude all the time when life has given you so many hard knocks?"

Thus, your excellent attitude has a lasting, positive effect on the people in your life. Their faith in humanity is renewed as they watch you overcome every challenge and remain excellent no matter what obstacles stand in your way. You make them feel a little better every time they leave your presence. As a result, they invite you to come deeper into relationship and fellowship with them.

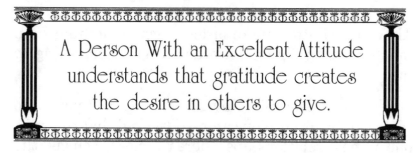

A Person With an Excellent Attitude understands that gratitude creates the desire in others to give.

When you're thankful, people just can't stop pouring into you. Why is that? They just want to see a demonstration of a grateful heart again!

Speaking from the standpoint of a husband, I'd have to say there is nothing better in life than a thankful woman. The only thing that transcends that is the Rapture!

Just ask any husband. He'll know what I'm talking about. If his wife asked him what would make him happy, he'd probably respond, "Just for you to be happy." Why is that? Because a wife can crush a husband with one look or make him a giant with one word.

Most wives have no idea how happy it makes their husbands to hear them cheerfully humming or singing around the home. A wife can bless her husband immeasurably just by saying to him spontaneously from her heart, "You know, Honey, you're the greatest!" That's so much better than listening to a wife who complains all the time! When a husband knows his wife is at peace and grateful for all he does for her, he starts looking for more ways to bless her.

A husband thinks nothing can be better in life than walking in the door every night to a wife who hugs him and tells him how important he is to her; how encouraged she is to be married to him; and how thankful she is that he has decided to lay down his life for her. It is very easy for a man to cherish and take care of a wife like that, because gratitude always creates a desire in a spouse's heart to give even more.

That's the same kind of response a grateful attitude generates in every area of life. A grateful person causes others to want to give to him. Once they see his happy, thankful heart, they just can't help it. They say, "Let me try this again. I want to give more to you!"

"But why do you keep giving to me?"

"Because I like to see the thankfulness that comes out of your heart when I do!"

"But I don't deserve this."

"That's one reason I like to give to you. Because you know you don't deserve it, so you're grateful. You don't know how rare it is to find a grateful person!"

That's exactly what a person with an excellent attitude is in this modern world — a rare and wonderful find!

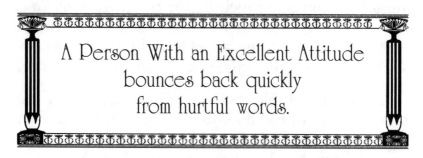

A Person With an Excellent Attitude
bounces back quickly
from hurtful words.

A person who has an excellent attitude doesn't really care what other people say to him. He bounces back easily from hurtful words because he is secure in *God's* love for him.

One time a man came up to me and said, "I hate you. Do you understand that? I hate you."

I reply, "No, you don't hate me. You just think you do."

"Yes, I do hate you!"

"No, you don't."

"How can you say I don't hate you?"

"Because you are a Christian, and Romans 5:5 says the love of God has been shed abroad in your heart by the Holy Ghost who been given to you. So you may think you hate me, but the love of God is inside you. You just need to let His love come out!"

I continued, "Besides, you don't even know me, so how can you hate me? You probably think you hate me because of something you heard about me that isn't even true. The person who told you probably didn't even know what he was talking about!"

All that man did when he became offended toward me was disqualify himself in God's eyes. He let that offense rob him of receiving what God wanted to give him. But the man didn't hurt me at all with his words because I know I'm accepted and beloved of the Father. I live in the knowledge that I'm the righteousness of God in Christ.

This is what a person with an excellent attitude understands. This is how he lives in his relationships with others. That's why he is able to bounce back quickly from words that would destroy others and walk free of hurt and offense, no matter what someone else says or does.

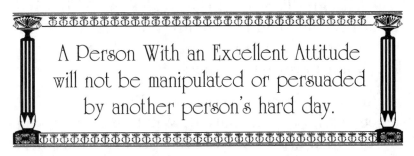

A Person With an Excellent Attitude will not be manipulated or persuaded by another person's hard day.

When someone you are interacting with is having a hard day, you should do all you can to encourage and lift up that person. As far as is possible with you, don't let him stay negative or discouraged. That way you'll be so focused on continually pumping him full of good that he'll never be able to take you down!

You see, a person with an excellent attitude just keeps speaking right words even when the people around him are speaking wrong words. He doesn't let others' moods or opinions affect him. He just keeps responding to everything that comes his way from God's point of view. That's why a person of excellence is always on top of the situation instead of the situation being on top of *him*.

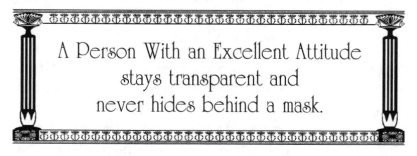

A Person With an Excellent Attitude stays transparent and never hides behind a mask.

It's interesting to me that so many Christians are hypocritical. These Christians live their lives speaking from behind an invisible mask. Behind that mask is the truth about themselves that they don't want to reveal to others.

But a person with an excellent attitude is someone who is transparent. What you see is what you get with a person like that because there is no mask to hide who he really is. Therefore, he doesn't have to go under construction — fasting and praying to make things right between him and God — before he can hold a conversation with you. He just stays simple, direct, and honest in all his relationships, especially in his relationship with God.

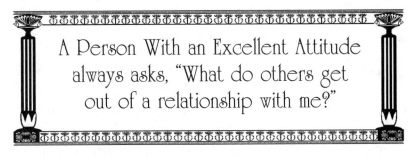

A Person With an Excellent Attitude always asks, "What do others get out of a relationship with me?"

The sad truth is, most people go through life with self-centered attitudes. Even in the Church, people have been taught to be self-centered.

Most Christians don't spend much time thinking about what's going on in other people's lives. In every situation they face, they think instead about how it will affect them. *What's going to happen to me if I do this?* they wonder. *What will I get out of it? What about me, me, me?*

Personally, I don't let myself think the thought, *What about me?* That thought never even crosses my mind anymore. Instead, I think about what the cost will be to the other people involved. You see, I know God will take care of me, so my attitude is never "What do *I* get out of this?" I'm not looking for a "win-win" situation in any of my relationships because I'm always striving for a "you win" situation.

People often say, "All my relationships have to be 'win-win' situations." But there really isn't any such thing.

There is no middle ground to find in a godly relationships. We have to constantly look for what we can give into our relationships rather than what we can get out of them; otherwise, those relationships will stagnate and eventually die.

You see, too many people try to hide behind a bunch of "maybes" in their relationships; meanwhile, they try to maneuver themselves to a place where they can put off to the future the decisions they need to make today. But that kind of compromise has no place in the Kingdom of God. That's why the Bible says, "Let your yea be yea and your nay be nay" (James 5:12).

Remember, friend, your attitude, whether excellent or poor, will cause you to live in the memory of your last encounter with each person you meet. So let me ask you this: *What is the mental snapshot the people in your life have of their last encounter with you?* What do they remember about being with you? What kind of impression did you last leave in their minds? Can they hardly wait to speak to you again? Does a smile come to their faces every time they think about you? Do they say, "That is a really nice person! I really like being around him [or her]."

If you're a person with an excellent attitude, that is exactly what people think about their last encounter with you. People can hardly wait to spend time with you again because you are so enjoyable to be around! They know that even though others may complain about their problems or look for what they can get out of a situation, you won't. You're too busy looking for what you can give into other people's lives. You're far too busy restoring people's faith in humanity with your excellent attitude!

PRINCIPLES FOR RELATING TO OTHERS WITH AN ATTITUDE OF EXCELLENCE

★ A Person With an Excellent Attitude draws others to himself for refreshing and for a renewal of faith in humanity.

★ A Person With an Excellent Attitude understands that gratitude creates the desire in others to give.

★ A Person With an Excellent Attitude bounces back quickly from hurtful words.

★ A Person With an Excellent Attitude will not be manipulated or persuaded by another person's hard day.

★ A Person With an Excellent Attitude stays transparent and never hides behind a mask.

★ A Person With an Excellent Attitude always asks, "What do others get out of a relationship with me?"

NOTES:

_____

_____

_____

_____

_____

NOTES:

ESTHER VS. VASHTI: APPROACHING AUTHORITY WITH AN EXCELLENT ATTITUDE

Long ago in the ancient land of Persia, the lives of two very different women intersected in a most unlikely way. One woman had great wealth, favor, influence, opportunity, and status at her disposal; yet in the end she lost it all. The second woman was born to a people in exile with none of the advantages that the first woman possessed. Yet in the end, the second woman gained all that the first woman had lost.

What was the source of these two very different outcomes? *Two very different attitudes.*

The names of these two women were Vashti and Esther, and their story is found in the book of Esther. I want to help you understand the differences between these two women so you can follow Esther's example of an excellent attitude — an example that leads to benefit and blessing rather than to loss and defeat. But before I share some of these differences, let me give you a little background information.

During the height of the Medo-Persian empire, a king named Xerxes, or Ahasuerus, reigned. By the third year of his reign, King Ahasuerus was already very successful. He possessed great riches and vast holdings of land. He had an army of servants to cater to his every need and desire.

Everything was going wonderfully for this king, so he decided to set aside six full months to show off everything he had accumulated to all the princes of the empire's provinces. He showed off his servants, his riches, his possessions, and his capital city of Susa. At the end of the six months, he held a great banquet not only for the princes and elders, but for all the people in the city. Meanwhile, Queen Vashti held her own banquet for the women of the palace.

On the seventh day of the banquet, the king said to his chamberlains, "I'd like you to call in Vashti. The people and the princes need to see how beautiful she is."

Now, I don't know where people have gotten the idea that the king wanted his queen to dance a perverted dance before his guests. The Bible doesn't say that. All it says is that she was fair to look upon and that the king asked her to show up at the banquet. He was proud of his beautiful wife, and he wanted to impress his guests with her beauty.

It's also important to understand that this was a fixed marriage rather than a love affair that resulted in marriage. It was Queen Vashti's job to show up when the king so ordered. However, Esther 1:12 tells us that the queen responded with a poor attitude when the king summoned her to his great banquet:

But Queen Vashti refused to come at the king's command brought by his eunuchs; therefore the king was furious, and his anger burned within him.

Queen Vashti's poor attitude and lack of respect cost her position as queen. Upon the advice of his counselors, the king banned her from his presence and sent out officers into all the provinces to gather the most beautiful young women in the land so he could choose a new bride. Esther, a beautiful young Jewess, was among the group of women chosen. And because of her excellent attitude, Esther was chosen above every other woman to be queen of the most powerful empire on earth at that time.

Let's look now at some of the differences in attitude between Vashti and Esther that caused the second woman to gain all that the first woman lost.

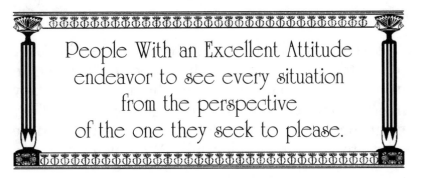

People With an Excellent Attitude
endeavor to see every situation
from the perspective
of the one they seek to please.

We can see a key attribute of a poor attitude in Vashti's refusal to comply with her husband's wishes. You see, people with a poor attitude are very subjective and self-centered. They refuse to consider anyone else's point of view; instead, they see every situation only from their own perspective. *What does this mean to me?* they ask themselves. *That's all I'm interested in.*

Because people with a poor attitude only see things from their own perspective, they are continually refusing to do what is asked of them by those to whom they are assigned. This is in direct contrast to people with an excellent attitude, who strive to understand their authorities' point of view in order to better serve them. People of excellence are interested not only in doing what they are asked to do, but in fulfilling their responsibilities to the best of their ability.

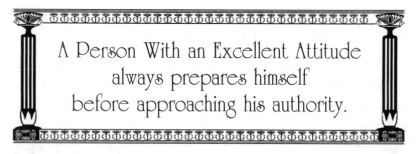

A Person With an Excellent Attitude always prepares himself before approaching his authority.

Esther prepared herself well before she ever attempted to converse with the king. This is an attribute of people with an excellent attitude. They always prepare themselves before they speak. They weigh out their words, not allowing inappropriate words to slip out accidentally. Whatever they say, they say on purpose because they know what they are saying is good and accurate.

This is a manifestation of the quality described in Proverbs 31:18 (*KJV*), referring to the virtuous woman: **"She perceiveth that her merchandise is good...."** This woman checked out her merchandise and concluded, "This is good." If it *wasn't* good, she was going to change it before anyone else ever graded it and said it was poor. In the same way, a person with an excellent attitude makes any necessary adjustments as a part of his preparation to approach the person to whom he is assigned.

That's what Esther did. You see, she didn't have the right to go before the king anytime she wanted to. She couldn't just come to him and say, "I feel like talking to you about this matter right now. Who are you to tell me that I can't?" Esther would have gained nothing by taking *that* approach.

No, Esther understood what she had to do. Therefore, she thoroughly prepared herself to approach the king — not only physically, but spiritually as well.

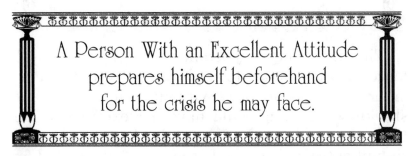

A Person With an Excellent Attitude
prepares himself beforehand
for the crisis he may face.

Esther didn't just assume that victory would be hers. She prepared herself so she would be ready for any crisis that might arise. In Esther 4:16, she told Mordecai:

"Go, gather all the Jews who are present in Shushan, and fast for me; neither eat nor drink for three days, night or day. My maids and I will fast likewise. And so I will go to the king, which is against the law; and if I perish, I perish!"

Esther was saying, "Everyone must fast and pray because I don't know what is coming." This young Jewess understood well the importance of preparation in order to receive favor from the person God has placed in authority. She was a rare woman indeed who continually displayed an excellent attitude.

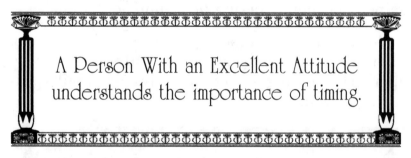

A Person With an Excellent Attitude understands the importance of timing.

Timing is very important to a person of excellence. Esther understood that. She was going to enter the king's presence without an invitation, and she knew the king could have her executed if her timing was off. But Esther 5:1,2 tells us of the successful outcome because Esther carefully waited for the proper time:

Now it happened on the third day that Esther put on her royal robes and stood in the inner court of the king's palace, across from the king's house, while the king sat on his royal throne in the royal house, facing the entrance of the house.

So it was, when the king saw Queen Esther standing in the court, that she found favor in his sight, and the king held out to Esther the golden scepter that was in his hand. Then Esther went near and touched the top of the scepter.

Esther waited for the right time and therefore received the favor of both God and the king.

We see in John 2 that Jesus also understood the importance of timing. When His mother Mary asked Him to change the water into wine at the wedding in Cana, He said to her, "My hour has not yet come" (John 2:4).

We have no better example than Jesus of someone who lived continually with an excellent attitude, so this statement of His is very significant to us. Jesus knew that timing was crucial to a successful outcome in every situation.

Understanding the importance of timing also includes recognizing when the timing is right in our own lives to move on to the next season. But we need to understand this: If we do not prepare before that moment comes, it will never happen. Our attitudes today set the future seasons of tomorrow.

A Person With an Excellent Attitude
complies from the heart.

Esther was able to gain audience with the king and rescue her people from destruction because of her attitude of willing compliance. On the other hand, Vashti was unwilling to comply with the king's wishes, adopting a defiant attitude instead. This is what the king's counselor advised him as a result:

> "For the queen's behavior will become known to all women, so that they will despise their husbands in their eyes, when they report, 'King Ahasuerus commanded Queen Vashti to be brought in before him, but she did not come.'
>
> "This very day the noble ladies of Persia and Media will say to all the king's officials that they have heard of the behavior of the queen. Thus there will be excessive contempt and wrath.
>
> "If it pleases the king, let a royal decree go out from him, and let it be recorded in the laws of the Persians and the Medes, so that it will not be altered, that Vashti shall come no more before King Ahasuerus; and let the king give her royal position to another who is better than she.
>
> **Esther 1:17-19**

So the king told Vashti in effect, "Okay, if you want to rebel, you can rebel. No one can stop you. But you have now disqualified yourself from being my queen."

That's one of the things about attitudes that most people don't realize. A person can be as rebellious as he wants, but he has to be ready to accept the consequences of his disqualifying attitude.

Now, you might read about Queen Vashti and say, "Vashti didn't really do anything wrong. She didn't deserve to lose her position as queen!" But remember, it doesn't matter what you and I think is wrong. It mattered what *the king* thought was wrong. He was the one with the power to "pull the plug" on Queen Vashti's position as his queen!

Besides, I can give you a good reason why Queen Vashti's refusal to obey her husband was so dangerous: *A poor attitude is contagious.* As the king's counselor said in Esther 1:17:

> **"For the queen's behavior will become known to all women, so that they will despise their husbands in their eyes, when they report, 'King Ahasuerus commanded Queen Vashti to be brought in before him, but she did not come.'"**

This man understood that a poor attitude is contagious. He knew that when the other women heard about the disrespectful way Queen Vashti had treated her husband, they would act the same way.

That's why we need to stay away from people with poor attitudes. You see, *we will act according to the lowest level of the people with whom we spend time.*

So who has God placed as the "king," or the authority, in your life, friend? Are you willing to obey that person from your heart?

Some people answer that question by saying, "Well, Jesus is the King in my life." That may sound good, but it only disguises their rebellious attitude if they are using that statement to discount the people God has placed over them in the different arenas of life.

If Jesus were truly the King in those people's lives, they wouldn't have a problem with obeying the laws of the land (Rom. 13:1-7) or honoring their mother and father (Eph. 6:1-3). They would also willingly obey their church leaders according to Hebrews 13:17:

> **Obey those who rule over you, and be submissive, for they watch out for your souls, as those who must give account. Let them do so with joy and not with grief, for that would be unprofitable for you.**

Notice that God *didn't* say in this verse, "If you want to and it feels all right to you, obey those who rule over you." The words "obey" and "want" don't go in the same sentence! An obedient attitude says, "I don't necessarily hold the same opinion about this matter that you do; nevertheless, I'll do what you ask me to do."

Many times people only pretend like they are complying with their authorities so that they can avoid being confronted about their rebellious attitude. But in reality, it's evident that they are complying only in action, not from their hearts.

You see, a person's excellent attitude isn't revealed merely by his act of obedience, but by his happy willingness to obey from his heart the person God has placed over him. If he decides to continually defy his authority, he leaves no recourse to that authority; the relationship has to be broken. But in that case, it wasn't the authority figure who broke the relationship; that person did it with his defiance.

Why is this true? Because the moment a person defies his authority, he gives up his right to determine the consequences for his defiance. He disqualified himself from having an opinion on that matter the moment he decided to demand his own way.

Let me put in another way. If I defy the authority God has placed over me, I can't go to that person afterward and say, "I've had a rebellious attitude toward you, but you're a Christian so you have to forgive me." No, I gave up my right to say that person should forgive me the moment I defied him. Why? Because I sowed seed that was outside the Word of God. Now I have opened myself up to reaping a harvest that is outside the Word of God.

Our children learn the truth of this principle when we as parents have to discipline them for doing wrong. They often want to tell you what kind of punishment they should get for their offense. "I promise I won't do it again, Dad. Please, just one swat!"

When my son Anthony would say that to me, I'd reply, "No, you're going to get three."

"Please, Dad, just one!"

"Okay, you can have four swats."

It didn't take long for Anthony to figure out that he had lost the right to determine the consequences for his misdeed and that he'd do better if he just stayed quiet and took his punishment!

In the same way, Vashti gave up her right to determine the consequences of her wrong attitude when she defied her husband. The minute she defied the king's wishes, she turned herself over to someone else's decision regarding her fate.

I'll tell you what — it's just better to get our attitudes right and to comply from the heart so we can stay in position for God's favor and blessing in our lives!

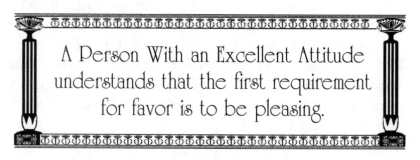

A Person With an Excellent Attitude understands that the first requirement for favor is to be pleasing.

I don't want the people with whom I have relationships to just endure me. I don't want them to go through all sorts of trials just to keep things on an even keel with me. I want to be a pleasing person to all the people in my life.

For instance, I love my wife Linda, and I've chosen to be pleasing to her. She doesn't have to beg me for it. She doesn't have to do anything to make me want to be pleasing to her. As an act of my own will, I continually look for ways to please her because it is my desire to be a pleasing husband.

I also want to please my superiors. I don't want them to have to ask me to do better at pleasing them. In fact, I never want those whom God has placed over me to have to correct me about anything. Now, if it becomes necessary for them to speak to me, I will receive their instruction without crying or trying to justify myself. But meanwhile, I will keep seeking to please them as much as possible.

Esther understood this principle very well. She studied how to be pleasing to her husband, the king. She actually did extensive research in order to know how to be what her husband needed. As a result, Esther gained access into the presence of the king — a place Queen Vashti could no longer go because she refused to be pleasing to her husband.

Now, Esther's achievement didn't happen overnight. It took about four years for the king to find someone who pleased him enough to be his new queen. During that four years, his servants traveled to 127 provinces, bringing back the most beautiful virgins out of all those provinces.

Every young woman who was selected eventually had the opportunity to spend time with the king. If he wasn't pleased with her, however, she was placed in the house of the concubines, possibly never to see the king again.

But Esther found favor with all those she came in contact with in the palace, including Hegai, the king's eunuch and custodian of the women:

> **Now the young woman pleased him [Hegai], and she obtained his favor; so he readily gave beauty preparations to her, besides her allowance. Then seven choice maidservants were provided for her from the king's palace, and he moved her and her maidservants to the best place in the house of the women.**

> **Esther 2:9**

Why did Esther encounter favor wherever she went? *Because an excellent attitude is pleasing not just to one, but to many.*

Most people are not willing to develop this quality in their lives. They think it is somehow condescending to become what another person needs.

But that is exactly what I want to do with my life. I don't want to be what *I* want to be. I want to be what someone else needs me to be. I'm not interested in doing what I want to do. I'm interested in doing what the person to whom I am assigned wants me to do.

"Yes, but don't you have any thoughts of your own?"

No, I don't. My thoughts are all centered around how to be pleasing.

Esther understood how to be pleasing. That's why she was the one chosen to become queen in place of Vashti. That's also why Esther became known as **"...the young woman who pleases the king..."** (Esther 2:4).

In the "house of women," the harem where the women waited for their audience with the king, Esther prepared for the moment she would be summoned for her time with the king. She had watched the other women get together and talk about what they were going to take with them when it was their turn to go in to the king.

But Esther didn't talk to the other women about how to win the favor of the king. She went to *another man* — Hegai, the king's eunuch and custodian of the women — and asked him what she should do to please the king.

In the end, the Bible says that Esther pleased the king more than all the rest put together. Why? Because she *studied* how to be pleasing.

The principle we can learn from Esther is this: *You must give a person what he doesn't require in order for him to be open about what he truly desires.*

If you go beyond someone's expectations, you will immediately find out that what he wants is actually very small. After all, you've already given him more than he would ever ask for!

I've had individuals come to me and ask, "Pastor Robb, what can I do for you?"

I reply, "Well, you can do so-and-so for me."

Then I find out later that these individuals forgot to do what I requested. Yet they still come back and tell me again, "I really want to do what you want me to do."

No, people like that *don't* want to do what I want them to do. If they really wanted to please me, they wouldn't forget to do what I've already asked of them. That just puts me in the position of having to correct them, which is definitely not a pleasing position to be in!

Esther wasn't like the individuals I just described. She understood that she had to give what the king didn't require in order to find out what he truly desired.

That's what you must do as well if you want to be known as a person with an excellent attitude. Focus on pouring goodness into the lives of those to whom God has assigned you. Make their needs more important than your own needs, and choose on purpose to be their problem-solver.

Once you turn your heart toward becoming pleasing to someone else, your life will be immediately begin to be enhanced — whether it's through a promotion at your job, a new sense of peace inside your home, etc. Maybe your spouse will suddenly get more excited about spending time with you, or perhaps your boss will unexpectedly decide he wants to give you a raise.

Whatever the result, the cause will be the same: *You decided to focus on pleasing others rather than on pleasing only yourself.*

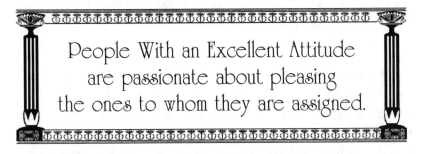

People With an Excellent Attitude
are passionate about pleasing
the ones to whom they are assigned.

Excellence means that the goal of pleasing those above you becomes not just your desire, but your *passion.* You see, the people to whom God has assigned you are the ones who can give you the opportunity to become all He has called you to be. You wouldn't be where you are now if it weren't for the people God has placed in front of you. Therefore, how far you go forward in life depends on the quality of your attitude toward your authorities and how well you learn to solve the problems they face.

I can use my own marriage as an example. If all my wife Linda did was give me a fit every day, how far do you think she and I would go in life? I guarantee you, not very far! Linda realizes that the responsibility of our future is based on her as much as it is based on me.

I'll say it another way: *The promotion of your future depends on the attitude you bring to the table.* When you maintain an excellent attitude, the person in front of you can concentrate on what God has called him to do instead of constantly having to turn around and fix what is behind him. That's important, because God never called those who are in front of you to fix your yesterdays; rather, you have been called to help solve their problems of tomorrow.

A person with a poor attitude wants to turn that around. He never attempts to please others; he just pleases *himself*. When Queen Vashti didn't go to the banquet according to the king's wishes, she was pleasing herself and refusing to please her husband. But in the end, her poor attitude cost her dearly. Selfishness always does.

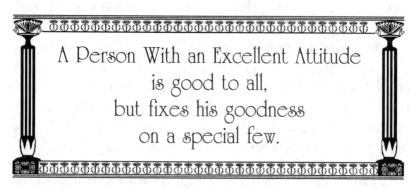

A Person With an Excellent Attitude is good to all, but fixes his goodness on a special few.

We must work consistently at being pleasing to the few to whom we have been assigned. If we spread ourselves too thin in our relationships with people, we will never have much of an impact on anyone's life, nor will we reap any worthwhile harvest from the seeds we've sown.

Think about it. If we never sow more than 1/8 inch deep in the lives of five thousand people, our harvest will only come from a crop that has 1/8-inch-deep roots. But suppose we decide instead to focus on sowing deep into the lives of five people to whom God has assigned us. In doing that, we could increase our harvest one thousand times!

That's why we need to focus our seed — our involvement in the lives of others for the purpose of blessing and benefit. Of course, we should love and be kind to everyone. But we should focus our efforts of being excellent on the few to whom God has assigned us.

I don't want to be excellent with everyone; I'm not striving to go deep with a lot of people. I just want to be excellent to a few.

I understand that someone is always watching me who is greatly able to change my future. And if that someone has to choose between a person who always sows 1/8 inch deep into his life and someone who is focused on sowing deep into his life, which one do you think he is going to promote? He will promote the one who has the desire to sow deep — the one who is willing to put the time, commitment, and energy into finding new ways to bless him and to solve problems for him.

That's important for you to know, for it helps explain why *it's better to be more to a few than to be less to many.*

But before you begin to focus your seed, consider this: *What qualities do you have that cause you to be noticed by others?* These are the qualities you should focus on as you seek to please those to whom God has assigned you. Remember, the qualities that make you different from others are the qualities that give you significance in their lives.

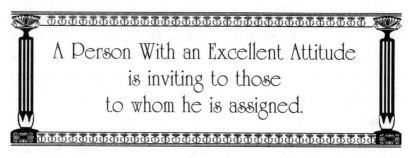

A Person With an Excellent Attitude
is inviting to those
to whom he is assigned.

Be inviting to the people you communicate with. Make sure everyone you come in contact with is blessed. That's how you promote yourself in a positive manner.

You see, people want happy communicators around them. They don't want someone around them who is more of a commitment than a pleasure to know. With that kind of person, it sometimes takes forty-five minutes to straighten out what he messed up in three minutes because his momma never taught him the right way to act.

This person was probably never spanked for his poor attitudes. Now the people close to him are continually catching the exhaust of those same poor attitudes just because someone didn't want to fulfill his or her responsibility in the past. And the people who have to endure this person's poor attitude today often haven't done a thing to deserve it!

Have you ever noticed that we take out our poor attitudes on the nicest people in our lives? After all, a mean person wouldn't let us get away with it. If we tried to take out our bad moods on a mean person, he'd just smack us silly! So unless we have learned to discipline our flesh, we have a tendency to find the nicest person we can take advantage of and then let our poor attitude take over.

That's where people got the idea that nice guys finish last. It was never supposed to be that way — and in God's Kingdom, it *isn't* that way. Esther 5:2 tells us that, in the case of the king's choice of a new queen, the nicest woman finished *first*:

> **So it was, when the king saw Queen Esther standing in the court, that she found favor in his sight, and the king held out to Esther the golden scepter that was in his hand. Then Esther went near and touched the top of the scepter.**

This verse tells us that *favor flows in our direction when someone is happy to see us.*

A wife might say, "I can't understand why my husband doesn't come home right after work." Well, maybe he doesn't come home for a reason.

Or a husband may complain, "I can't understand why my wife always cries." Maybe she cries for a reason.

Marriage partners just need to ask themselves this question: *Does my attitude toward my spouse invite or repel communication?*

Esther approached the king in a way that invited communication. Thus, even though the king hadn't summoned her, he stretched out his scepter to her and asked her what she desired. Esther then began her plea for the lives of her people by saying, **"If I have found favor in the sight of the king, and if it pleases the king to grant my petition and fulfill my request..."** (Esther 5:8).

Why did Esther say this? *Because pleasing our authorities is the requirement for receiving favor.* Favor doesn't come into our lives until we give those who are over us what they desire.

We often make the mistake of expecting others to be pleased with what we want to give them rather than what they actually want us to give them. Just think about the number of birthday and Christmas presents people receive that they never use!

Personally, I have received about thirty-five "pastor mugs" over the years. At this point, I need someone to give me a cabinet instead of another mug so I have a place to store them all!

But in order to gain significance in the lives of others, we must be willing to give others what they desire, not what we want to give them. This is how we obtain favor in their sight and become known as people with excellent attitudes.

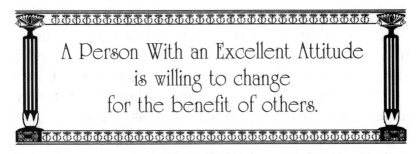

A Person With an Excellent Attitude
is willing to change
for the benefit of others.

If I see something I need to change in my life in order to benefit others, I'll change in a minute. I want to become everything my superiors want me to become. I don't allow myself to even consider the excuse, "Oh, that's just the way I am."

This is the very attitude that has made so many married couples miserable for so long. Some couples are seventy-five or eighty years old, have despised each other for decades, and yet are still saying to each other, "You'll have to accept me just the way I am." These same couples often say with a certain sense of pride, "Well, at least we've stayed together all these years."

When I hear that comment from this kind of married couple, I tell them, "Are you kidding? You haven't been together for the last forty years! 'Together' means you have your home in divine order. It means you're doing what the Word says and that you're willing to change for the benefit of your marriage. 'Together' *doesn't* mean that even though you get in your respective 'tanks' every day and shoot at each other, you don't blow each other up!"

A person with a poor attitude lives continually with the attitude, "Take me the way I am, or leave me. I'm not changing for anyone!" For instance, in the workplace, this person might agree to change anything in order to get a particular job. But then after he gets hired, his supervisor asks, "Listen, could you please change this about yourself?" Suddenly the new employee has a poor attitude!

The new employee tells his supervisor, "I can't believe you want me to change! You need to just accept me the way I am."

"But I don't like this particular characteristic of yours."

"Then why did you hire me?"

"That's simple — I didn't know you very well before I hired you!"

This happens a lot in life. People wait until they're safe and secure in a job, in a marriage, in a friendship, and so forth, before they begin to show who they really are. Then they get offended if someone who is in close relationship with them tries to examine them or help them correct their faults. They say, "If you were really my friend, you wouldn't ask me to change."

"No, I am your friend, and that's why I'm telling you that you need to change — because if you don't change your behavior in this area, we won't be able to be friends anymore."

"What do you mean by that? I don't think you truly love me."

"The very fact that I'm willing to tell you the truth proves that I love you."

"Then why do you insist that I change?"

"Because I don't have any disposable relationships. I want a lifelong relationship with you, and I'm telling you what you need to do in order to make sure that comes to pass."

(Can you tell I've had this very conversation with more than one person in the past? I have to continually keep in mind what Proverbs 27:6 says: **"Faithful are the wounds of a friend...."**)

In contrast, a person with an excellent attitude understands that love is the very reason his superiors ask him to change. Therefore, he is willing to accept greater examination from the people God has placed over him. Knowing that they have committed themselves to him, he therefore trusts their judgment.

The truth is, when we love someone with whom we have relationship, we should be willing to change for that person's benefit. Otherwise, we are demonstrating that we only love ourselves. Love must always be our motivator on the job, in our homes, with our friends, and in our interactions with the world. If someone close to us explains the benefit he will receive if we alter ourselves in some way, we need to pray about the matter and be willing to change if the Lord confirms it to our hearts.

We may want to protest, "But people need to accept me the way I am!" That isn't necessarily true. Do our actions contradict our confession? If we want to be everything our superiors need us to be, there can be no refusal in us to change.

"But I can't believe he would ask me to do that!"

I'll tell you what we *can* believe: God will deliver us from any situation that could ultimately harm us. Meanwhile, He loves us so much that He wants to help us stop sowing rebellion into the atmosphere. You see, He knows that seeds of rebellion are destined to return to us as a harvest of negative consequences in the future. This is why we must always stay willing to change if we want to live as people of excellence.

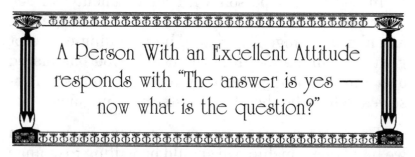

A Person With an Excellent Attitude responds with "The answer is yes — now what is the question?"

Do you want to make sure that you receive all the blessings God intends for you to enjoy through the people He has placed over you? Well, this is a key principle for achieving that goal. (Of course, this principle presupposes that the authority respects his relationship with you too much to ever request something unscriptural or unreasonable from you.)

When we live before our authorities with an excellent attitude of servanthood and love, we'll enjoy every benefit possible from those relationships as we grow into a deeper, closer fellowship. On the other hand, if we make our authorities "requalify" every day for the right to speak into our lives, we will have relationships that are only one day deep and a thousand days long.

This is often the problem in many marriage relationships. For instance, a wife may make her husband continually requalify by proving his love for her. But how many days in a row should a husband have to tell his wife he loves her before she believes he does? If a wife has a difficult time believing that her husband can love her, it's a sure indication that she doesn't really believe God loves her either.

I never want to make the people requalify whom God has placed over me. I believe what they tell me. I'm not going to say, "Well, now, did you really mean that?"

Too many Christians make God requalify His love for them on a daily basis and therefore never enjoy what He has already said is theirs. They don't enjoy the inheritance God has given to them in Christ Jesus because they still don't believe it is theirs. They don't realize that God's blessings are right in front of them, ready for them to pick up and receive by faith. Even when they read His promises in the Bible, they say, "Well, I'm not so sure that's true for me."

I've decided I'm not going to make that mistake. I'm going to enjoy the benefits God has already said are mine. I'm also going to believe in the people He has placed over me, maintaining the attitude that says yes before a question is even asked. I know that's the way I can ensure God's blessing on my life in the future.

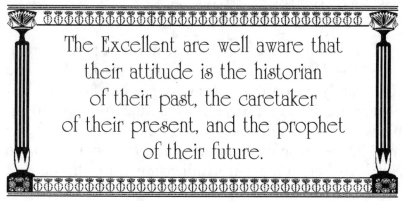

The Excellent are well aware that their attitude is the historian of their past, the caretaker of their present, and the prophet of their future.

In contrast, a person with a poor attitude doesn't consider the future consequences for his rebellious words or actions. This was Queen Vashti's downfall. If she had known she was going to lose everything, she would have gone to that banquet. But she didn't count the cost of the consequences. Her heart betrayed her, and her poor attitude disqualified her from future blessing, for the king gave her royal position to someone else who was better than she (Esther 1:19).

You see, our attitudes originate from our *hearts*. This is why we must determine never to con people; otherwise, sooner or later our hearts will betray us.

So work on improving the condition of your heart, friend. Give your allegiance to God through a good attitude and the faith-filled words of your mouth. When you do that, no man will ever be able to take away from you the benefits and blessings you receive from God!

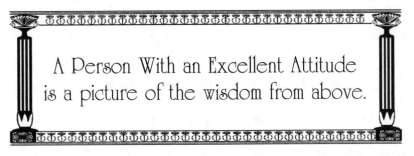

A Person With an Excellent Attitude
is a picture of the wisdom from above.

A person with an excellent attitude is a living example of what the Bible calls "the wisdom that is from above." James 3:13-17 tells us what this divine wisdom looks like:

> **Who is wise and understanding among you? Let him show by good conduct that his works are done in the meekness of wisdom.**
> **But if you have bitter envy and self-seeking in your hearts, do not boast and lie against the truth.**
> **This wisdom does not descend from above, but is earthly, sensual, demonic.**
> **For where envy and self-seeking exist, confusion and every evil thing are there.**
> **But the wisdom that is from above is first pure, then peaceable, gentle, willing**

to yield, full of mercy and good fruits, without partiality and without hypocrisy.

Notice that verse 17 says a person with a truly good attitude is never a hypocrite. He doesn't display a good attitude in front of people and then start criticizing and complaining behind their backs. Verse 18 goes on to say he goes through life as a peacemaker:

Now the fruit of righteousness is sown in peace by those who make peace.

On the other hand, the person with a poor attitude is an unhappy person. His unhappiness has nothing to do with the situations he faces in life. He's just an unhappy person to begin with. Verse 16 tells us why:

For where envy and self-seeking exist, confusion and every evil thing are there.

A Christian who walks through life with a poor attitude is confused and in strife within himself. He knows what to do, but he doesn't do it. He says he believes the Word, but he doesn't act on it. He says he loves God, but other things hold his attention. He says God is first place in his life, but everything else comes before Him. And the list goes on and on.

This is why a person with a horrible attitude is ultimately replaced by someone who is happy just to be there. A poor attitude is a chore to deal with, but it's easy to put up with a person who lacks talent if he's always happy. In fact, an employer might hire someone else for his talent and still keep the person who is always happy on staff just because he likes to be around someone like that! As Proverbs 28:14 says, **"Happy is the man who is always reverent** [respectful].**"**

I hope I never come to a place in life where I think I am irreplaceable. The moment I think I can't be replaced is the moment I'm in trouble. That's why I go through life just happy to be wherever God sends me. I don't think, *Oh, no, I have to do this again.* No, I'm just glad I can be a blessing in every situation I find myself in.

Vashti was replaced because of her poor attitude. The king took his counselor's advice:

"If it pleases the king, let a royal decree go out from him, and let it be recorded in the laws of the Persians and the Medes, so that it will not be altered, that Vashti shall come no more before King Ahasuerus; and let the king give her royal position to another who is better than she."

Esther 1:19

In our modern society, we are very hesitant to say that one person is better than another one. But the Bible says here that Esther was better than Vashti, and it all centered around the quality of each woman's attitude. Esther always maintained an attitude that reflected the wisdom from above. This is the kind of excellent attitude that will always come out on top in the end.

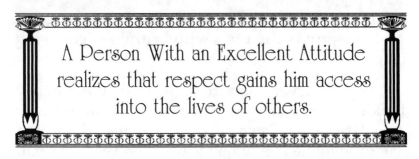

A Person With an Excellent Attitude realizes that respect gains him access into the lives of others.

When we show respect to those in authority over us, they will ask us to come closer. Esther understood that. Her uncle Mordecai sent her the message, "You have to go in and see the king about his decree to destroy the Jews." But she said, "I can't just go in unsummoned and unannounced. There is a proper way to approach the king."

Esther had respect for the king's position. She didn't just walk in the throne room and say, "Okay, King, we slept together a month ago, so now I have the right to come in here and talk to you." She prepared herself to approach the king in respect. And because she did, he asked her to come closer. She had found favor in his sight.

God has a way that He wants to be approached, too, but that's something most Christians never learn. For the most part, the modern American church has presented God only as a "Daddy God." But God is the Almighty King as well, and He desires to be approached as such. Psalm 100:4 confirms this:

"Enter into His gates with thanksgiving, and into His courts with praise...."

America is one of the only societies on the face of the earth that has no knowledge of a monarchy. American Christians don't understand what a king is, nor do they understand the concept of a king's word being absolutely final. Therefore, they tend to treat God with the contempt of familiarity.

The King invited us to intimacy, but instead of treating that intimacy with respect, we became too familiar with Him. We began to enter His throne room on roller skates, jumping on Daddy God's lap, and saying, "Just wrap your arms around me, Jesus!"

Do you know that America and perhaps Europe are the only places on the face of the earth where Christians lack a sense of protocol and respect when it comes to approaching God? None of the rest of the world takes God for granted like that. But wherever people show a lack of respect to God, their intimacy with Him suffers. Yet these same people often don't even realize that God has moved away from them. They think they're in the middle of the throne room of God, but they're actually still outside playing in the playground!

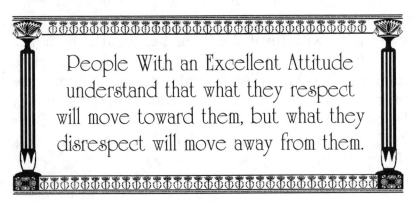

People With an Excellent Attitude understand that what they respect will move toward them, but what they disrespect will move away from them.

This principle explains why respect gives us the right of access to a person's heart. A person who sees our excellence will move toward us because he wants to take a closer look. But if that same person sees a lack of respect in our lives, he will turn away and think, *I certainly don't want to be near people like that!*

This principle certainly holds true in marriages. A lot of divorced couples claim that their broken marriage resulted from conflict over money. But it isn't money that causes divorces; divorce is almost always the result of poor attitudes.

When a spouse continually has a poor or disrespectful attitude toward the other marriage partner, he or she creates a situation in which there seems to be nowhere else to go and no other recourse but divorce. On the other hand, if a spouse is consistently loving, forgiving, embracing, and submitting his or her heart continually to the other marriage partner, no one is going to walk away from that!

This factor of *attitude* will even supercede the factor of *appearance* in a marriage. For instance, a man will walk away from a gorgeous woman who is great to be with until she opens her mouth and starts speaking a constant barrage of negative words. Both men and women will eventually distance themselves from spouses who put more confidence in the way they look than in the way they are. No wonder the Bible says that charm is deceitful and beauty is fleeting (Prov. 31:30)!

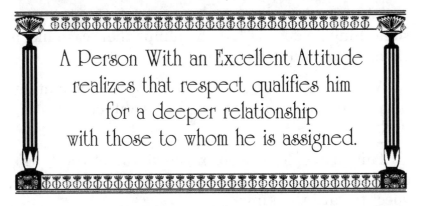

A Person With an Excellent Attitude
realizes that respect qualifies him
for a deeper relationship
with those to whom he is assigned.

I've never seen it fail. When I have shown respect to a person, I have always been invited into a deeper relationship. You see, I never allow myself to take a person for granted. I posture myself in such a way that I am always the student; I am always the one who is willing to learn. From that position of respect, I am invited deeper into the life of that person with whom I have entered into relationship.

Some of my friends have told me, "We've been friends for a while now. I want you to begin to take some things for granted in this friendship because we've grown so close."

But I won't do that. I will not be buddies with my friends. I have determined never to take advantage of a friendship or to cross the line that leads to the contempt of familiarity. I'll never get over my respect of people.

A person with a poor attitude has no such conviction. He is no respecter of persons. He doesn't have a poor attitude toward just one person; he has a poor attitude toward everyone! Even the people he likes can be the brunt of his disrespect. If they say something he doesn't like, he jumps their case like a chicken on a June bug!

As a result, this person's disrespect affects many people, not just the person he is directly dealing with.

This principle is seen in the words of the king's counselor regarding Queen Vashti's display of disrespect toward the king:

"...Queen Vashti has not only wronged the king, but also all the princes, and all the people who are in all the provinces of King Ahasuerus."

Esther 1:16

This is why it's so vital to maintain an attitude of excellence. Only when we are respectful of the people to whom God has assigned us will we be invited into a deeper relationship with them.

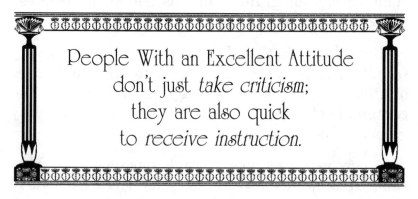

People With an Excellent Attitude
don't just *take criticism*;
they are also quick
to *receive instruction.*

When Esther was first brought before the king, she didn't tell him that she was a Jewess. Why not?

Because she was quick to receive instruction from the man who had raised her:

Esther had not revealed her people or family, for Mordecai had charged her not to reveal it.

Esther 2:10

Now, the Bible says that Mordecai was the nephew of Esther's mother. That means Esther had been taught how to live life by her cousin! Even after she became the queen, Esther continued to receive instruction from Mordecai. In her new position, she could have had him killed before the sun went down, but instead she remained teachable because she had an excellent attitude.

On the other hand, a person with a poor attitude is stubborn. I see this quite often in churches, in businesses, in marriages, and in friendships.

Stubborn people are no fun to be in relationship with. Their stubbornness shows just how little they think of others. The only thing that is important to them is what *they* want. They love their own opinion more than they care for those who try to instruct them.

That doesn't ever have to describe you, friend. You can decide to stay teachable, no matter what — always quick to receive instruction from those whom God has placed over you in authority.

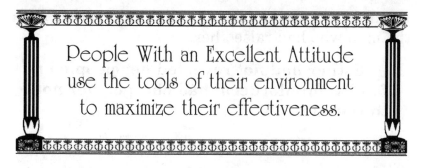

People With an Excellent Attitude use the tools of their environment to maximize their effectiveness.

As Esther prepared for her time with the king, she underwent a regimen of soaking first in oil of myrrh for six months and then in beautifying perfumes and spices for another six months. This was her time of purification, during which she got rid of everything that was detrimental to her and added all she could that was beneficial to her. How did Esther do this? *She used the tools of her environment to maximize her effectiveness.*

As I mentioned earlier, props were provided in the king's house of women so each woman could choose what she wanted to take with her when it was her turn to spend time with the king:

> **Thus prepared, each young woman went to the king, and she was given whatever she desired to take with her from the women's quarters to the king's palace.**

> **Esther 2:13**

Esther took full advantage of this provision, but not in the same way the other women did. Instead, she used great wisdom to determine which tools within her environment would enhance her relationship with the one she was to give herself to.

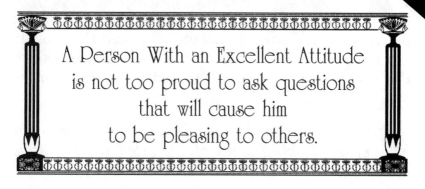

A Person With an Excellent Attitude
is not too proud to ask questions
that will cause him
to be pleasing to others.

People with a good attitude aren't too proud to ask questions that will cause them to succeed. This is what Esther did. Yes, she used the tools in her environment to enhance her relationship with the king, but she didn't choose those tools without help. She was willing to ask the advice of someone else who was more knowledgeable than she was on the subject of pleasing the king:

Now when the turn came for Esther the daughter of Abihail the uncle of Mordecai, who had taken her as his daughter, to go in to the king, she requested nothing but what Hegai the king's eunuch, the custodian of the women, advised. And Esther obtained favor in the sight of all who saw her.

Esther 2:15

The rest of the young women took the props they wanted from the house of the women when they went to the king. But notice what Esther did. She didn't make that decision on her own. She humbled herself and asked for advice from Hegai, the king's custodian of women. She asked him, "How do I get

properly? How do I get to the front of the
ow do I take a shortcut through the crowd?
I m interested in what *I* think pleases the king.
I'm asking you what *you* think I should take in order
to please him."

*Esther understood that she would never succeed
by giving the king what she wanted him to have
instead of what he wanted her to give him.*

So many people make that mistake. They give
the person they're assigned to what they want to
give him and then when he tries to correct them,
they say, "How can you say that after all I've done
for you?"

"I'll tell you what you've done for me. You've
given me a headache!"

Let me help you here, friend. An employee could
be the greatest worker that an employer has ever
had. But the moment the pain that employee brings
becomes greater than the problems he solves is the
moment the employer will distance himself from
him.

The same holds true in every area of life. That's
why I don't ever take anything for granted in my
relationships with those over me in authority. I keep
a very low profile. I don't enter a conversation with
them thinking I know anything; rather, I enter with
humility and meekness.

I always posture myself with my face bowed to
the ground in respect, ready to receive whatever
counsel and wisdom my superiors want to give me.

After all, I know I can't fall very far when I'm already face down on the ground! I also know that the moment I get a lofty idea about myself is the moment I *will* fall — and I intend to succeed in life, not fall on my face!

A Person With an Excellent Attitude
is openly loyal.

There is no question about where a person with an excellent attitude stands because he is openly loyal in his relationships with others.

So many Christians are not loyal in their relationships. For instance, I've actually had people who, while staying as guests in my home, went out to dinner with individuals who had publicly attempted to discredit me in the eyes of others. Even more amazing to me is the fact that my guests thought nothing of doing such a thing. They never even considered how I might feel about it.

When a person with whom I have a close relationship does something like that, where does he stand in that relationship? Well, I believe relationships are like a light switch; they are either on or off. There is no "dimmer switch" — with some relationships having a little more light and others having a little less light. No, either the switch is on, or the switch is off. A person is either loyal, or he is not loyal. It's that simple.

Esther was openly loyal to the king. Esther 2:22 talks about the time Mordecai learned of a plot to kill the king. As soon as Mordecai informed Esther of the plot, she informed the king:

So the matter became known to Mordecai, who told Queen Esther, and Esther informed the king in Mordecai's name.

Esther said, "King, I'm willing to stake everything I am on this report. I am loyal to you. Mordecai is loyal to you. We are on your side." As a result of the loyalty of Esther and Mordecai, the assassination plot was aborted and the king's life was spared.

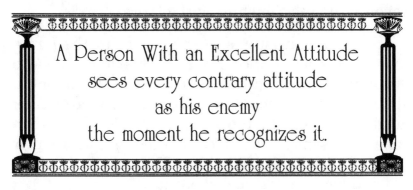

A Person With an Excellent Attitude sees every contrary attitude as his enemy the moment he recognizes it.

When we deal with our own poor attitudes as soon as we recognize them, we encourage others to straighten up *their* poor attitudes.

Just think back to your childhood for a moment. When your older brother or sister received a spanking, what happened to you and your other siblings? You all straightened up, didn't you? The older sibling got spanked, and everyone else adjusted their behavior. You all learned from watching the guilty one receive the punishment he or she deserved.

That's what the king's counselor was talking about in Esther 1:20:

"When the king's decree which he will make [against Vashti's rebellious act] is proclaimed throughout all his empire (for it is great), all wives will honor their husbands, both great and small."

In the same way, if we make a practice of immediately dealing with every poor attitude that arises in *our* lives, we will cause everyone around us to improve in *their* attitudes as well.

I don't know about you, but I want to pass this attitude test for real instead of going around the same mountain again and again, one poor attitude after another, day after day after day. However, whatever I achieve in this arena of attitude, I want to do it through God. Otherwise, it wouldn't be real and it wouldn't last.

I'm interested in receiving true promotion from God in my life. I want the real thing. I don't want to pretend like I have my act together when I don't. I want to be free of all pretension, but I don't want anyone else doing it for me.

I'm not interested in living a life in which I continually displease those in front of me. I don't want to blame everyone else for my own feelings of depression. I'm not going to spend my time thinking, *If only they were different — if they'd just get their act together, if they could just recognize my gift, if they could just see in me what I know is in me — maybe then life would be different for me.*

People don't need to see anything inside of me. I'm showing everyone all they need to know about me on the outside through my attitudes. That's why I've decided to deal with every one of my poor attitudes as soon as I recognize it. I'm determined to be known as a person with an excellent attitude every day for the rest of my life!

The story I've shared with you in this chapter is about two women with two very different attitudes. However, it doesn't matter what gender or color you are or where you grew up. The scriptural principles still apply to you, for all distinctions disappear in Christ Jesus.

So this is my question to you: *Which attitude are you going to adopt for your life — Vashti's or Esther's?* Your ultimate success largely depends on your answer to that question, for the attitude you carry into each situation of life is often the key that determines the outcome.

Therefore, I urge you to make a quality decision to become a person with an excellent attitude. Get serious about dealing with your poor attitudes as soon as you recognize them. If you've been thinking someone owes you something just for waking up in the morning, let go of that wrong thinking and start becoming a problem-solver for the people to whom God has assigned you.

As you choose to follow Esther's example of excellence, I can assure you of this: Your life will begin to be greatly enhanced the moment you turn your heart toward pleasing someone else other than yourself. Remember, when you rule your attitudes, you rule your own heart, opening the way for God to make winning an everyday event!

PRINCIPLES FOR APPROACHING AUTHORITY WITH AN ATTITUDE OF EXCELLENCE

★ **People With an Excellent Attitude endeavor to see every situation from the perspective of the one they seek to please.**

★ **A Person With an Excellent Attitude always prepares himself before approaching his authority.**

★ **A Person With an Excellent Attitude prepares himself beforehand for the crisis he may face.**

★ **A Person With an Excellent Attitude understands the importance of timing.**

★ **A Person With an Excellent Attitude complies from the heart.**

★ **A Person With an Excellent Attitude understands that the first requirement for favor is to be pleasing.**

★ **People With an Excellent Attitude are passionate about pleasing the ones to whom they are assigned.**

★ A Person With an Excellent Attitude is good to all but fixes his goodness on a special few.

★ A Person With an Excellent Attitude is inviting to those to whom he is assigned.

★ A Person With an Excellent Attitude is willing to change for the benefit of others.

★ A Person With an Excellent Attitude responds with "The answer is yes — now what is the question?"

★ The Excellent are well aware that their attitude is the historian of their past, the caretaker of their present, and the prophet of their future.

★ A Person With an Excellent Attitude is a picture of the wisdom from above.

★ A Person With an Excellent Attitude realizes that respect gains him access into the lives of others.

★ People With an Excellent Attitude understand that what they respect will move toward them, but what they disrespect will move away from them.

★ A Person With an Excellent Attitude realizes that respect qualifies him for a deeper relationship with those to whom he is assigned.

* People With an Excellent Attitude don't just *take criticism*; they are also quick to *receive instruction*.

* People With an Excellent Attitude use the tools of their environment to maximize their effectiveness.

* A Person With an Excellent Attitude is never too proud to ask questions that will cause him to succeed with others.

* A Person With an Excellent Attitude is openly loyal.

* A Person With an Excellent Attitude sees every contrary attitude as his enemy the moment he recognizes it.

NOTES:

_____

_____

_____

_____

_____

_____

_____

_____

_____

QUOTATIONS ON ATTITUDE

Here are some thought-provoking quotations by unknown authors on the importance of our attitudes:

I may not be able to change my world
around me,
but I can change the world
within me.

We cannot direct the wind,
but we can adjust the sails.

If you think you are beaten, you are.
If you think you dare not, you don't.
If you'd like to win, but think you can't,
It's almost certain you won't.
Life's battles don't always go
to the stronger or faster man,
But sooner or later, the man who wins
is the man who thinks he can.

It's your *attitude*, not your *aptitude*,
That will determine your *altitude*.

A pessimist is a person who,
regardless of the present,
is disappointed in the future.

We cannot continually behave
in a manner that is inconsistent
with the way we see ourselves.

Quitting is a permanent solution
to a temporary problem.

There is no wrong side of the bed;
we get up on the wrong side of our *minds*.

Never look back
unless you want to go that way.

You never get ahead of anyone,
as long as you are looking
to get even with them.

I'm not sure all happy people
are generous,
But I've never seen a generous person
who wasn't happy.

Attitudes determine *actions*.

You are not what you think.
What you think, you are.

It is unfortunate when people
allow themselves to get like concrete —
All mixed up and permanently set.

Confession of Faith For an Excellent Attitude

I have an attitude of excellence, and I am growing in the Lord. I'll be different tomorrow than I am today, for I am changing from glory to glory and from one level of excellence to the next.

I will allow God by His Spirit to continually motivate me to become better, rise higher, and achieve more than I ever have before. I will approach each situation with an excellent attitude and every relationship with a desire to please!

I'm going to go further. I'm not going to quit. I'm going to press on. I'm going to press through. I am going to reach for God's highest. I'm going to be everything He has called me to be!

PRAYER OF SALVATION

Perhaps you have never been born again and therefore haven't even begun the pursuit of excellence in God. If you have never received Jesus Christ as your personal Lord and Savior and would like to do that right now, just pray this simple prayer:

Dear Lord Jesus, I know that I am lost and need Your forgiveness. I believe that You died for me on the Cross and that God raised You from the dead. I now invite You to come into my heart to be my Lord and Savior. Forgive me of all sin in my life and make me who You want me to be. Amen.

If you prayed this prayer from your heart, congratulations! You have just changed your destiny and will spend eternity with God. Your sins were forgiven the moment you made Jesus the Lord of your life. Now God sees you as pure and holy, as if you had never sinned. You have been set free from the bondage of sin!